poems and paintings by

Douglas Florian

harcourt, inc.

ORLANDO • AUSTIN • NEW YORK • SAN DIEGO • TORONTO • LONDON

zoo's who

www.HarcourtBooks.com

Library of Congress Cataloging-in-Publication Data
Florian, Douglas.
Zoo's who: poems and paintings/by Douglas Florian.
p.   cm.
1. Animals—Juvenile poetry.   2. Children's poetry, American.   I. Title.
PS3556.L589Z66   2005
811'.54—dc22   2004004576
ISBN 0-15-204639-9

First edition

A C E G H F D B

MANUFACTURED IN CHINA

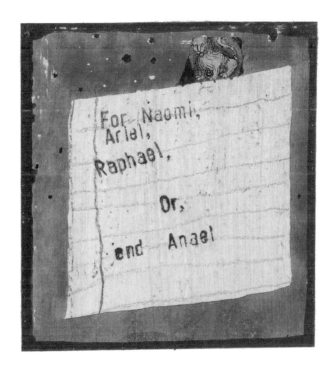

Contents

The Lizards

Lizards laze
And lizards bask.

What's their favorite food?
Don't ask!

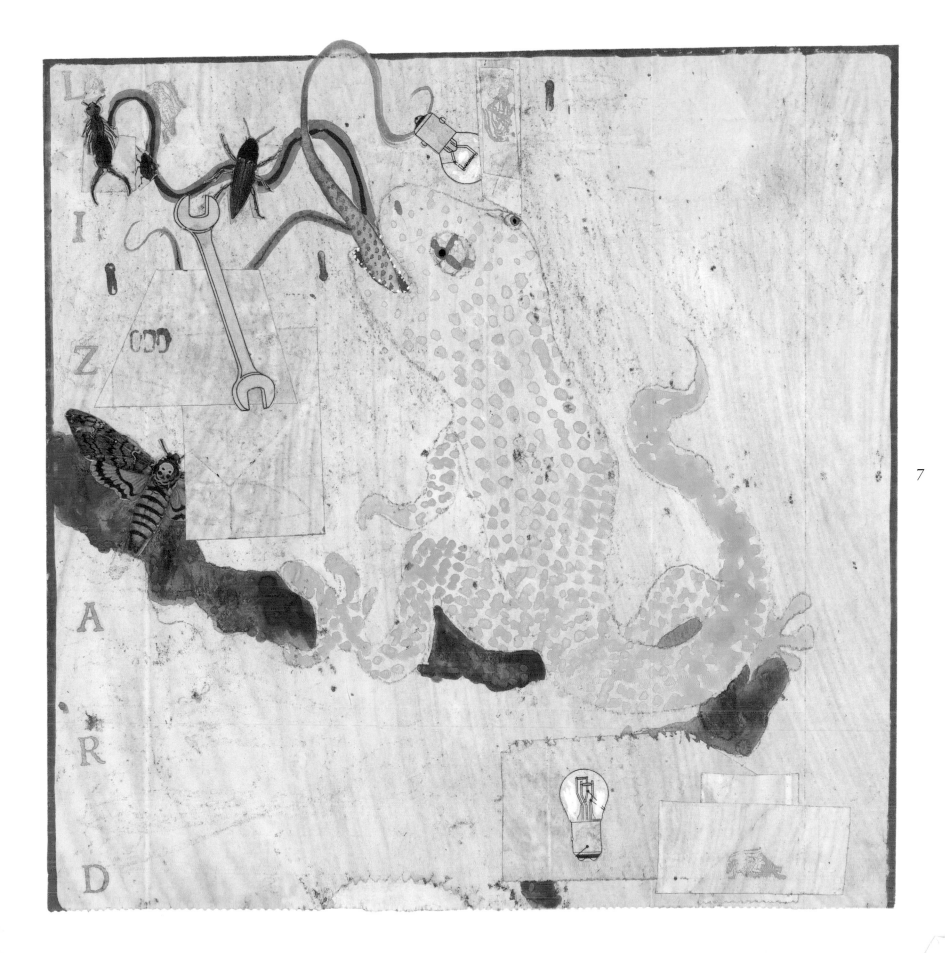

7

The Eagle

I'm not a seagull.
I'm royal.
I'm regal.
All birds are *not*
Created eagle.

The Manta Ray

The massive manta ray
Always has the right of way.

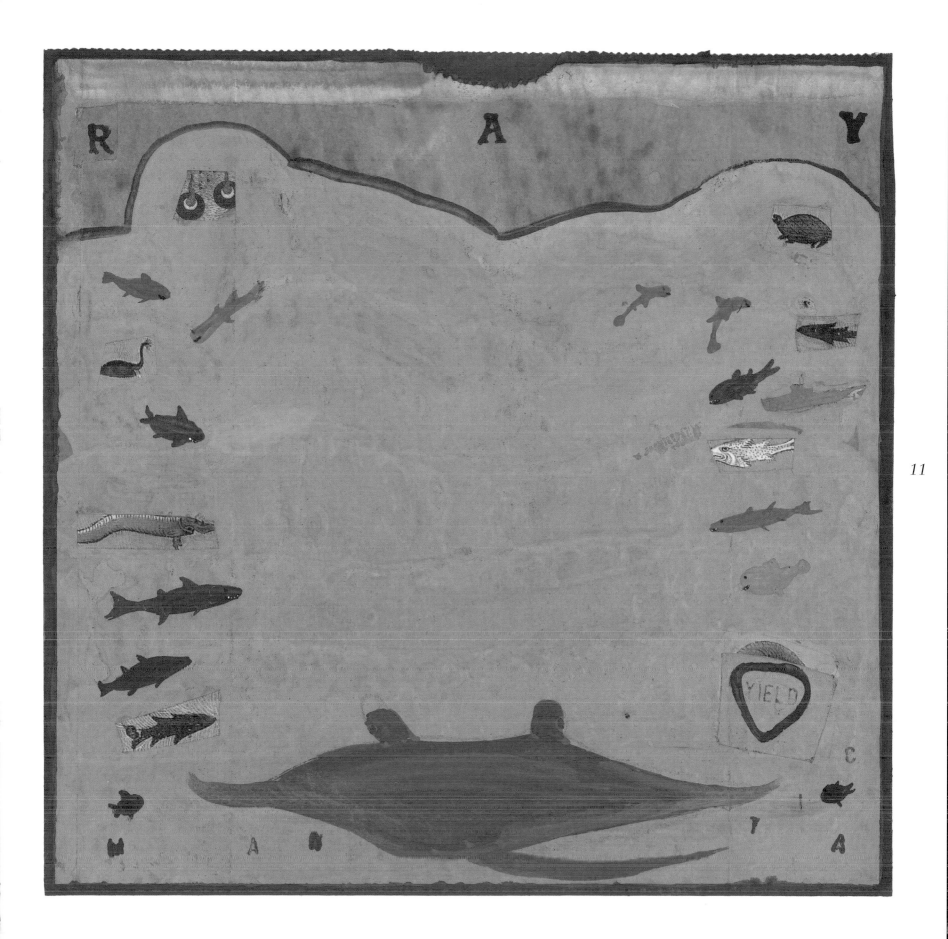

11

12

The Penguin

A penguin isn't thin—it's fat.
It has penguinsulation.
And it toboggans through the snow
On penguinter vacation.
The penguin's a penguinsome bird
Of black-and-white fine feather.
And it will huddle with its friends
In cold, penguindy weather.

The Bush Baby

Bushy back.
Bushy knees.
Bushy bush babies climb trees.
Bushy tail.
Bushy tush.
Oh baby, you're a bush!

15

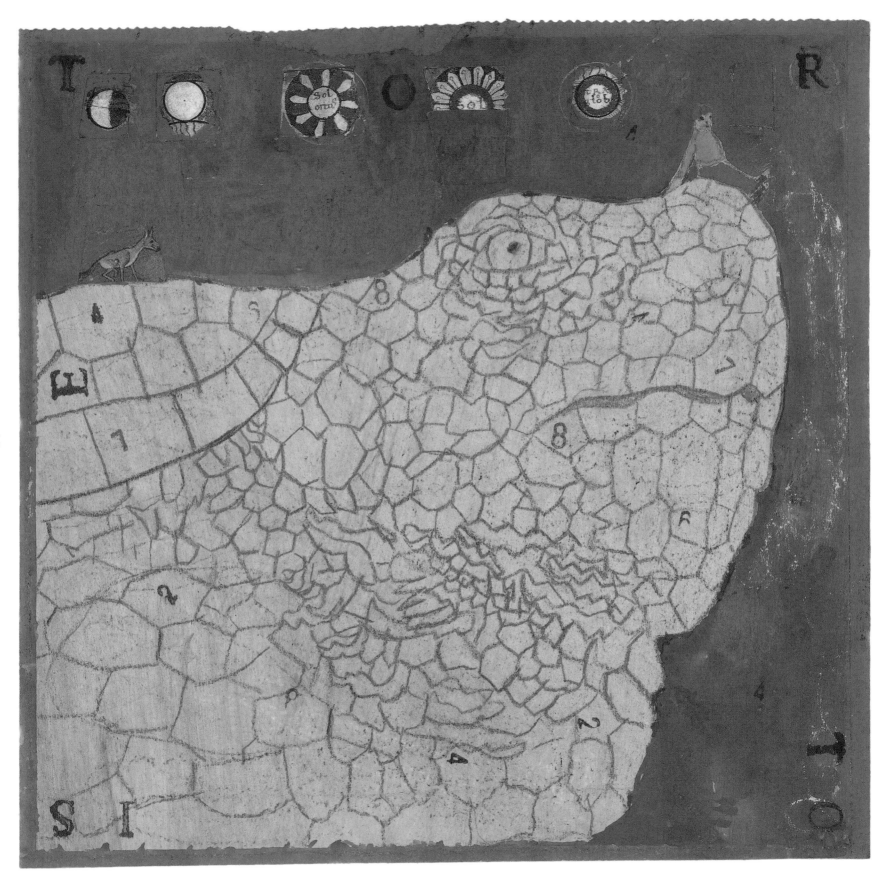

The Tortoise

Patience.
Persistence.
The will to endure.
The tortoise
Has taught us
All this
And more.

17

The Ladybugs

Some have four spots.
Some have seven.
Some have six spots.
Some eleven.
Some have two spots.
Some have ten.
Some are ladies.
Some are men!

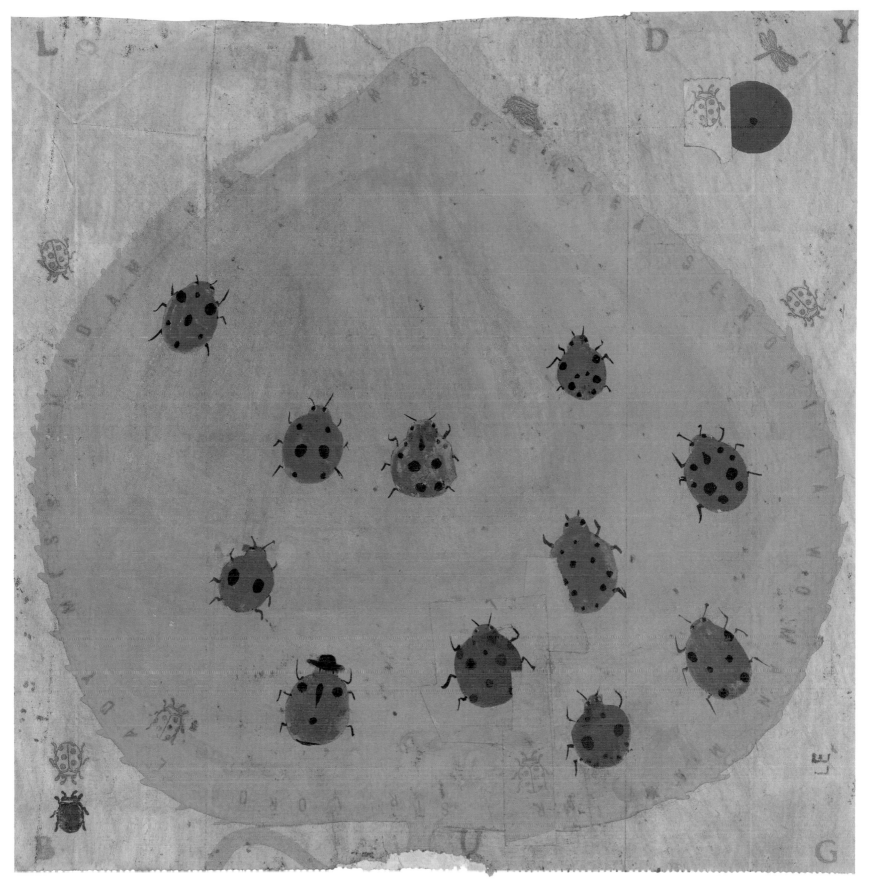

19

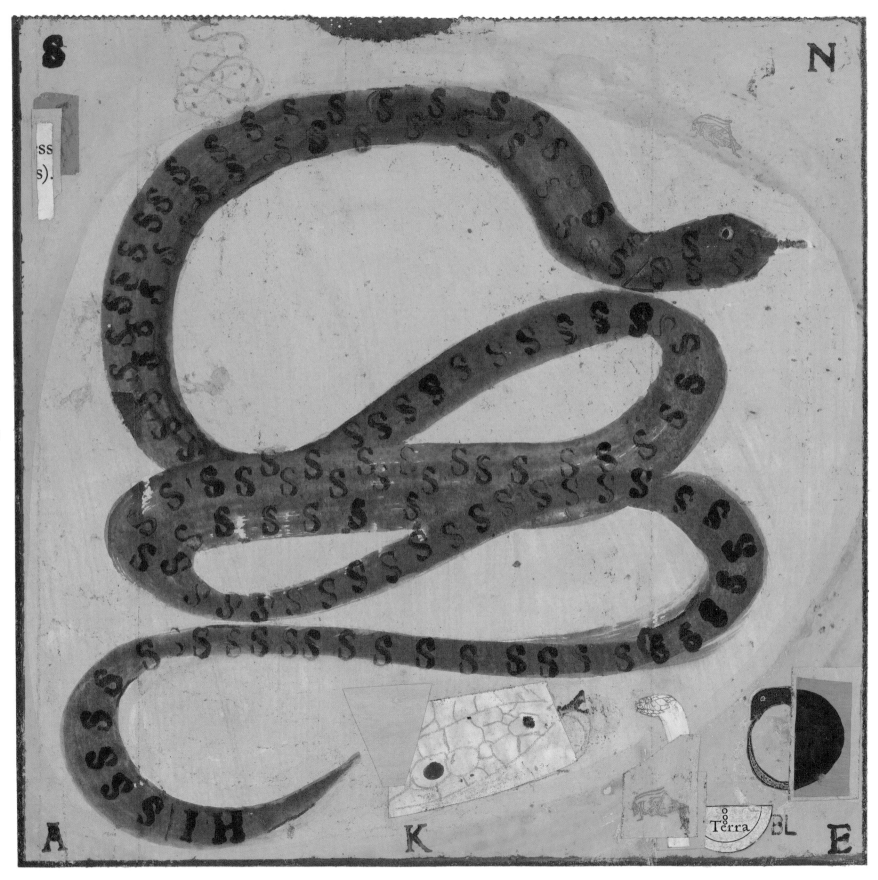

The Snake

A hissssing sound
On ground
I make:

Sssssssssssssssssssssssssssssnake.

The Sharks

Sharks grow sharp teeth
Row by row.
Some above and some below.
Some grow left, and some grow right.
Oh, and by the way,
Sharks bite!

22

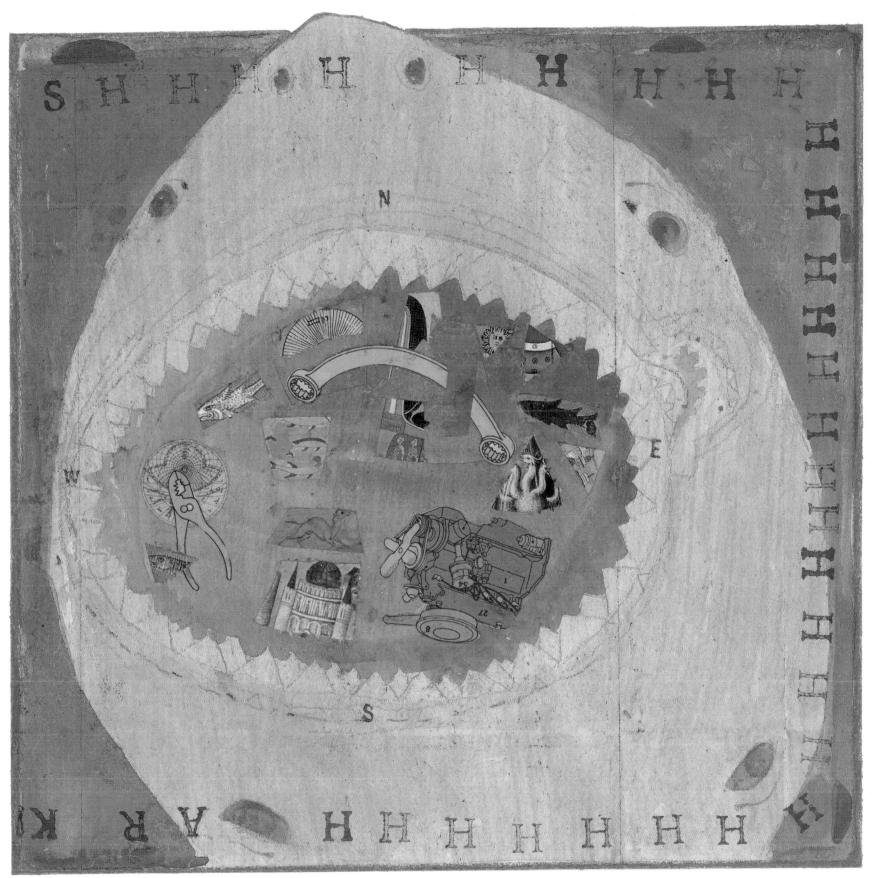

23

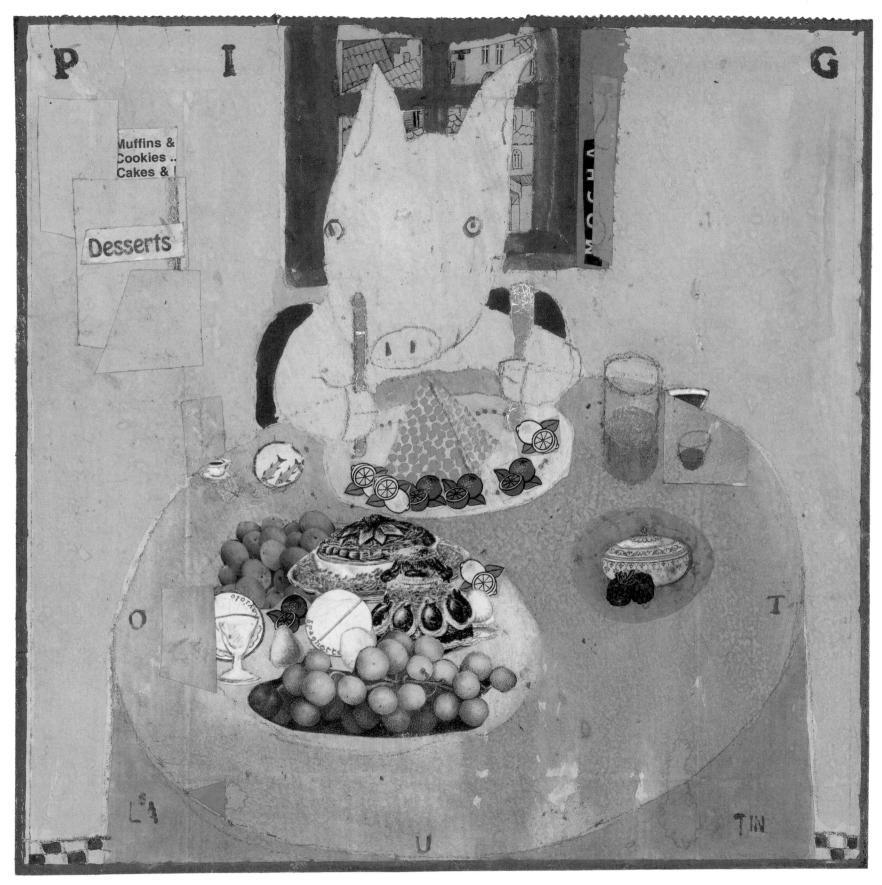

The Pigs

Pigs are portly.
Pigs are stout.
Pigs are big on eating out.

The Bats

In dark caves
So dank and dreary,
Bats, I hear,
Are very ear-ie.

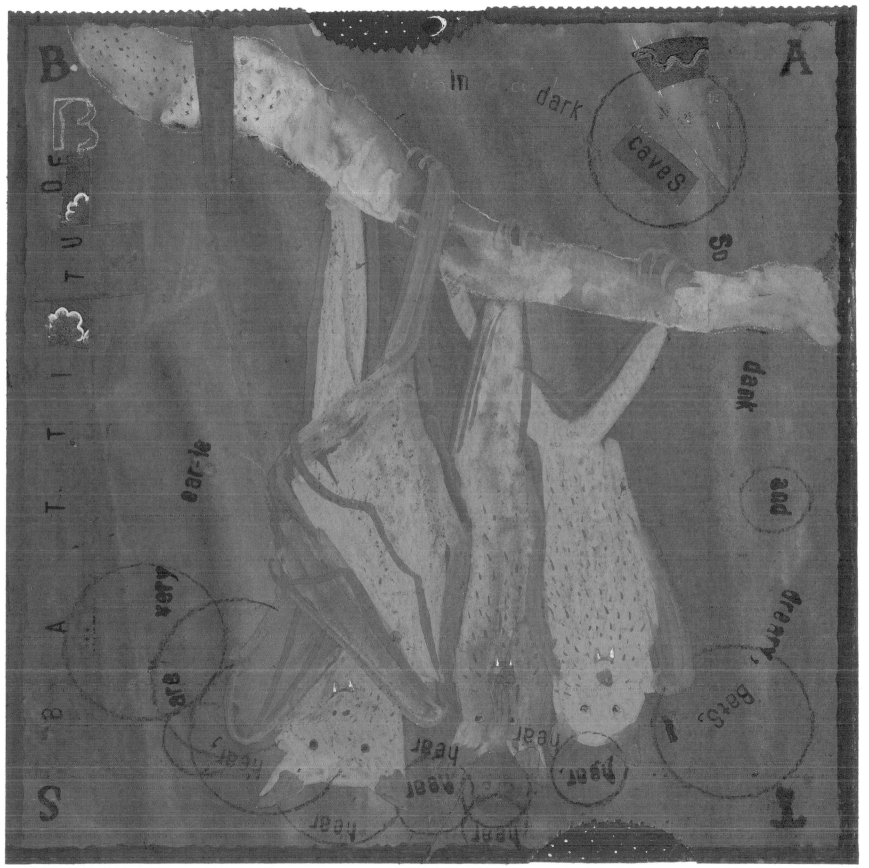

27

28

The Puffin

A puffin loves stuffin'
Its bill full of fishes.
It fills it with seven
Or eight if it wishes.
It always finds dishes
Of fishes delicious.
A puffin loves stuffin'
Its bill full of fishes.

The Slugs

Slugs are ugly.

Slugs are lowly.

Slugs climb mountains

Very slowly.

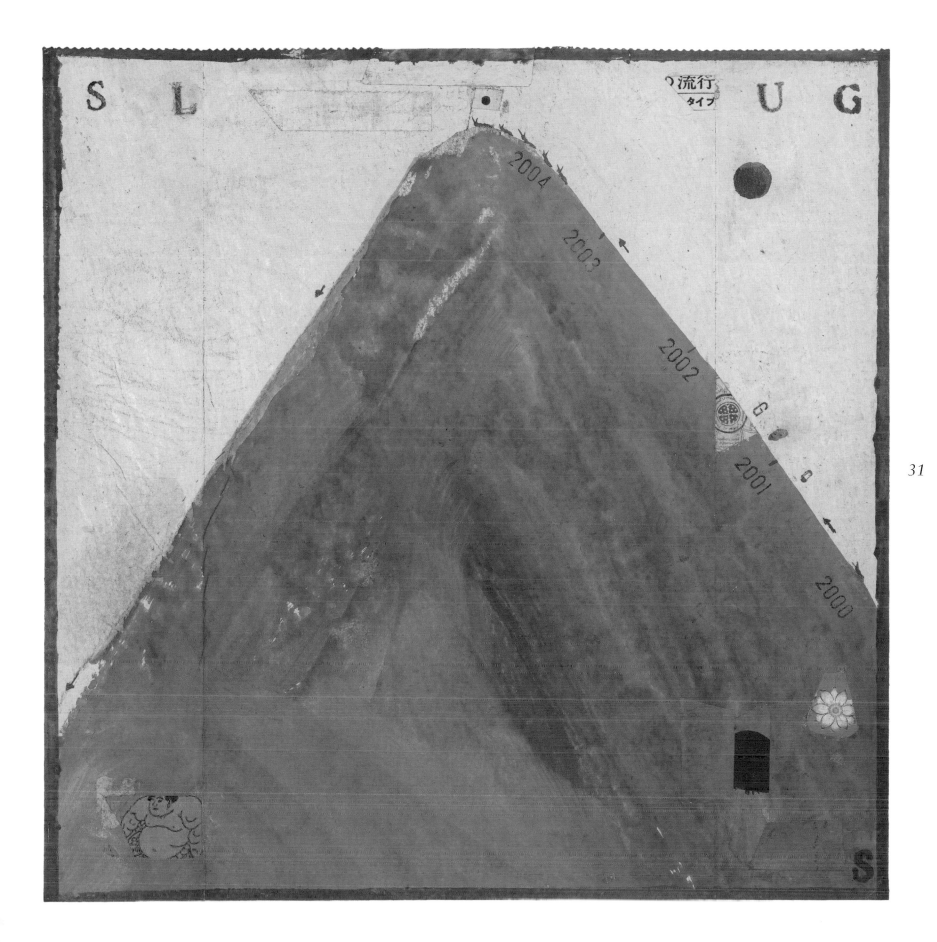

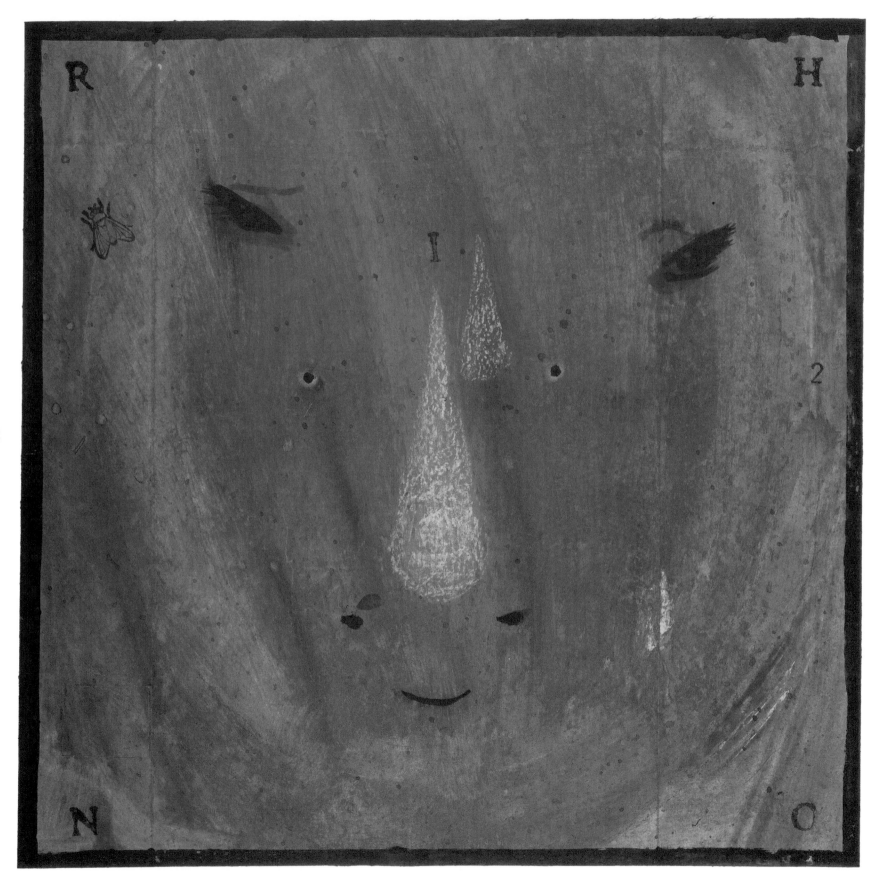

The Rhino

The rhino wallows in the mud.
He bathes in yucky muck and crud.
And though that doesn't make him cleaner,
It's wonderful for his demeanor.

The Terns

Terns turn left, and terns turn right.

Terns take turns at learning flight.

Terns, in turn, learn from each other.

One good tern deserves another.

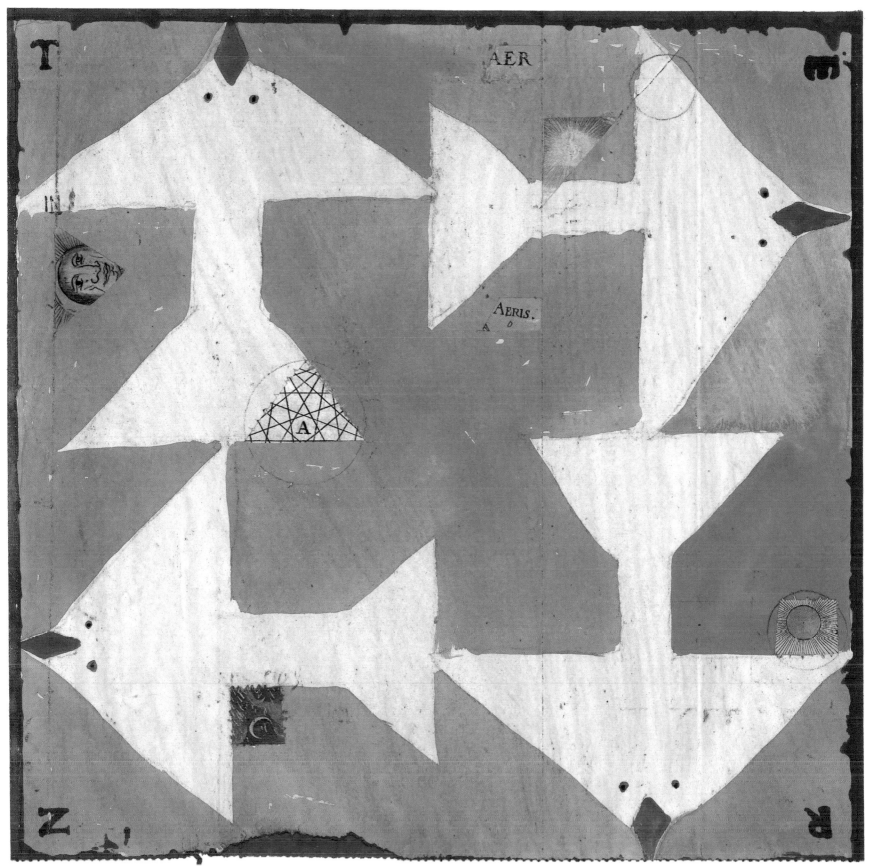

35

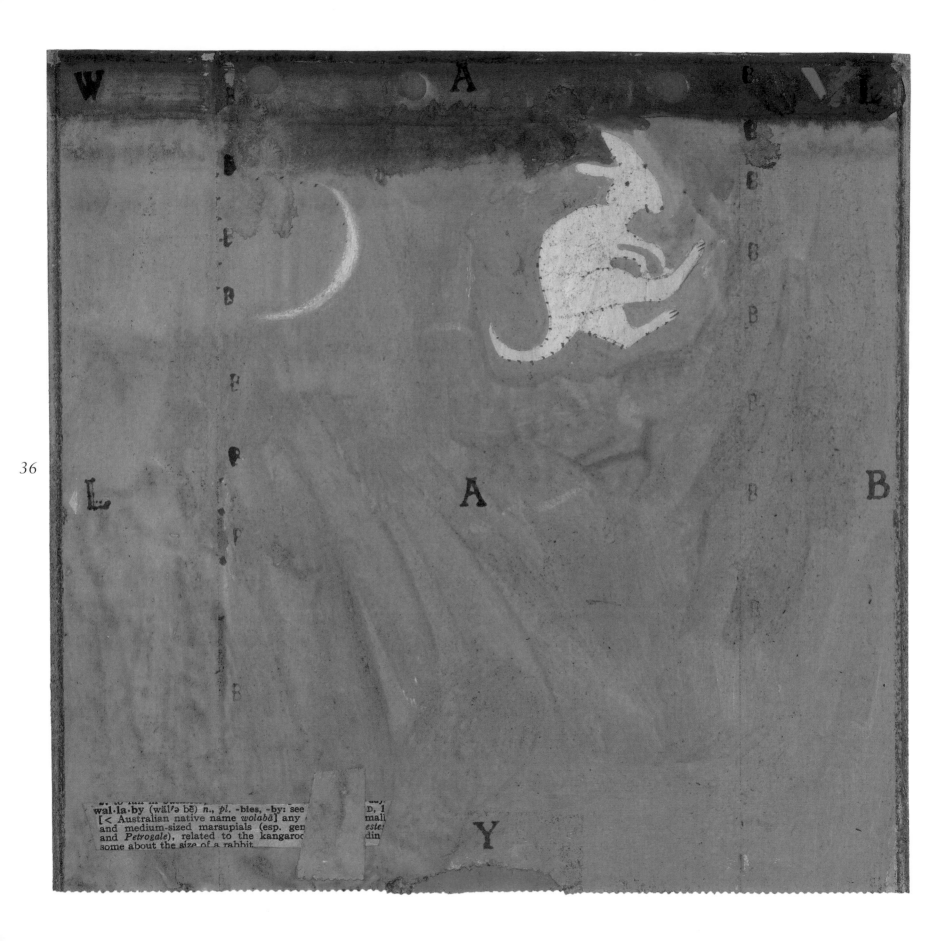

36

The Wallaby

Walla-be-nimble.
Walla-be-spry.
Walla-be-agile.
Leap for the sky.
Walla-be-lively.
Walla-be-light.
Walla-be-gravity-free
And take flight.

The Ant

I wANTed to write
A poem on an ANT.
I'm frANTic—
I cAN'T.

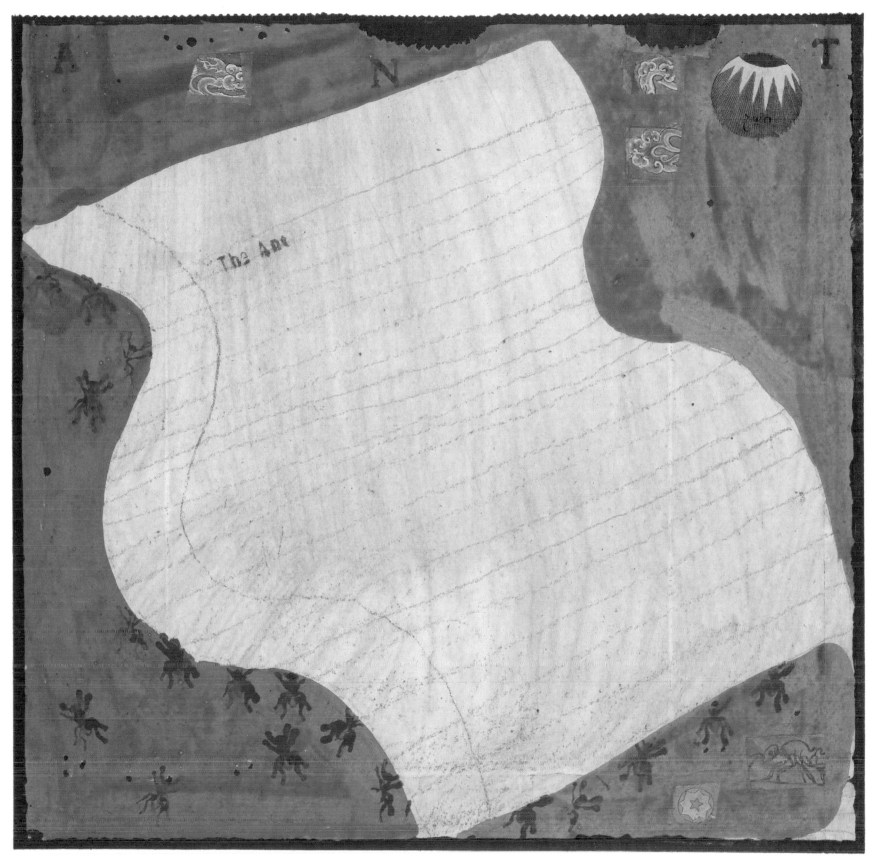

The Ant

39

The Sloth

Up a tree you slowly creep,
Then twenty hours straight you sleep.
Hanging from claws, each sharp as a knife.
Hey, sleepy sloth: Get a life!

The Shrew

A smallest mammal is the shrew.

It's eensie-weensie.

Teensie, too.

43

The Owl

I am the eyes
    And ears of night.
They say I'm wise—
    I say they're right.
On voles and moles and mice I'm fed.
A word to the wise—
Stay in bed!

The Sheep

Count on us
To fall asleep . . .
Shhhhhheep.

47

The illustrations in this book were done with watercolor, gouache,
colored pencils, inks, tin foil, candy wrappers, shredded papers, stencils,
rubber stamps, and much collage on primed brown paper bags.
The display type was set in P2 1722 Roman.
The text type was set in Sabon.
Color separations by Bright Arts Ltd., Hong Kong
Manufactured by South China Printing Company, Ltd., China
This book was printed on totally chlorine-free Stora Enso Matte paper.
Production supervision by Wendi Taylor
Designed by Ivan Holmes and Douglas Florian